Dots and Polka Dots

The Laidlaw Reading Program LEVEL 5

William Eller

Kathleen B. Hester

S. Elizabeth Davis

Thomas J. Edwards

Roger Farr

Jack W. Humphrey

DayAnn McClenathan

Nancy Lee Roser

Elizabeth M. Ryan

Ann Myra Seaver

Marian Alice Simmons

Margaret Wittrig

Patricia J. Cianciolo, *Children's literature*

David W. Reed, *Linguistics*

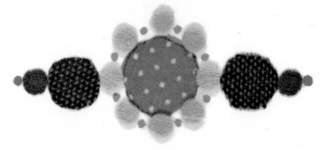

LAIDLAW BROTHERS · PUBLISHERS
A Division of Doubleday & Company, Inc.

RIVER FOREST, ILLINOIS

Irvine, California   Chamblee, Georgia   Dallas, Texas   Toronto, Canada

Acknowledgments

Follett Publishing Company for the poem *The Power Shovel* from THE DAY IS DANCING, copyright © 1968, by Rowena Bennett. Used by permission of Follett Publishing Company, a division of Follett Corporation.

Harper & Row, Publishers, Inc. for "Animal Tracks." Adapted from HOW TO BE A NATURE DETECTIVE by Millicent Selsam. Text copyright © 1958, 1963 by Millicent Selsam. Reprinted by permission of Harper & Row, Publishers, Inc.

The Saturday Evening Post Company, Inc. for the poem *The Magical Shoe* reprinted with permission of JACK AND JILL Magazine. Copyright 1972, The Saturday Evening Post Company, Inc.

Project Director: Ralph J. Cooke
Senior Staff Editor: Austin Tighe
Production Director: LaVergne Niequist
Senior Production Editor: Sonja Sola
Production Editor: Mary Ann Sullivan
Art Director: Gloria Muczynski
Art Consultant: Donald Meighan
Cover Art: Donald Charles
    Illustrators: Boecher Studios, Corinne and Robert Borja, Ralph Creasman, Len Ebert,
            John Faulkner, Paul Hazelrigg, John Mardon, Donald Meighan, Melinda
            Murakami, Tak Murakami, Carol Nicklaus, Barbara Olshewsky, Joe
            Rogers, Bill Shires, Carol Stutz, Lorna Tomei, Betty Wind
Photographers: Dan Miller (pp. 47–52, 54); Tak Murakami (pp. 32–35, 77);
            Larry Trone (pp. 100, 101, 102)

ISBN 0-8445-3158-8

Contents

6

8

Draw pictures to show the funny play.

Millie: I didn't sleep
for 10 days.

Tillie: Aren't you sleepy?

Millie: No, I sleep nights.

What would you call the story?

Act Out

Ben pulled and pulled.
Bill pulled and pulled.

"Wow!" said Ben.
"It sure is hard work
to pull this bed in the door."

"In!" yelled Bill.
"I'm trying
to pull it out!"

a Play

Woman: Do you like going to school?

Boy: Oh, I like the going—
and the coming back. But . . .

Woman: But what?

Boy: It's the time in between
that I don't like.

Letters, Letters, Letters

Make a letter hat.

Take a letter.

Draw it.

Cut it out.

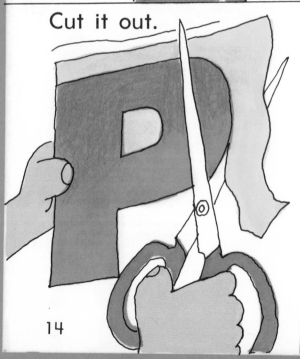

Wear it.

14

Be a letter person.

Tell the names of things that have your letter.

Clothes   Things that fly

Food   Things to ride on

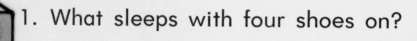

Who Knows?

1. What sleeps with four shoes on?

2. Can you write **I see you** in three letters?

3. Rudy took his monkeys for a walk.

   There were two monkeys

   before a monkey.

   And two monkeys

   after a monkey.

   And one monkey in the middle.

   How many monkeys did Rudy have?

   Do you know?

   Look on page 19.

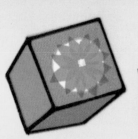

My Magical Shoe

Orange and green,
Yellow and blue,
Those are the colors
Of my magical shoe.

I love it
And it loves me.
With a snap of my fingers
It changes—one, two, three,

To purple and brown,
Silver and gold.
My magical shoe
Never grows old.

Michael Gluckman

Find a Rhyme

What could you do
With a magical shoe?
Could you bring it to a cat
And let her have it for a _ ?
You could tell it to hop,
But are you sure it will _ ?
You could tell it to fly,
But would it go up in the _ ?

Could you put it on your head,
Or play with it in _ ?
Could you color it brown,
And run all over _ ?
Just what would you do
With a magical shoe?
Just what would you do?

Were You Right?

1. A horse

2. I C U

3. Three monkeys

Look and see

Two monkeys before a monkey

Two monkeys after a monkey

One monkey in the middle

The Magical Broomstick

Andy put the last straws
in his Halloween broomstick.

"That's it!" he said.
"The straws look good
on a yellow broomstick.
Now I can fly on Halloween."

Andy hopped into bed.
Soon he was fast asleep,
dreaming of Halloween witches
and broomsticks.

And then —

right into his room

came four witches

on broomsticks —

singing,

With yellow and you!
And my broomstick, too.
Fly away to Cat Land!
Way above the moon!

Out the window went the witches

on their broomsticks.

Up into the sky.

Above the moon!

"Hop on your broomstick, Andy.

Nothing can stop us,"

called the last witch.

As she went out the window.

Andy grabbed his special broomstick.

He hopped on it.

Then he began to sing—

With yellow and you!
And my broomstick, too.
I'll fly away to Cat Land!
Way above the moon!

Zoom!

Sooner than you could say—

WiggleWitch

Andy was flying
with all the witches.
On their way to Cat Land.

Andy and the witches went flying,
right to King Cat's castle.
In Cat Land.
Above the moon.

"Stop!" yelled the big cat
guarding the castle door.
But the witches did not stop!

Right into the castle
they flew.
Into a big, big room
went the witches.
There King Cat sat.
He was a big black cat
with big green eyes!

Andy saw—
Some tiny black cats.
Some not-so-tiny black cats.
And some big black cats.

Round and round
the cats walked—
singing,

With yellow and you!
And my broomstick, too.
It's Halloween time
In Andy's Land!
Down below the moon!

Then King Cat called in a big voice,
"To your broomsticks, cats!
Let's fly!
To Andy's Land.
Below the moon!"

Andy jumped back on his broomstick.
Out into the sky he went,
right after King Cat!

Then came—
big cats, tiny cats,
enough cats to fill the sky.
Flying on their broomsticks—
down to Andy's Land,
down below the moon!

Then wham!
Andy came down
with a bang!

"Time to get up!
Time to get ready,"
Andy's mother called.
"It's Halloween!"

"You don't say," Andy answered
from down below his bed.
"You don't say!"

30

What Do You See?

Which cat has the widest mouth?

Look at the big black cat.

Is its hat
as *wide*
as it is tall?

ME Day

Betty: Hey, Kevin!

Why so sad?

Kevin: I want a day.

Betty: A day.

Did you say you wanted a day?

Kevin: That's right.

Just about everyone has a day.

So why not me?

Betty: Kevin, what are you talking about?

Kevin: Well, there's a Mother's Day

for mothers.

And a Father's Day for fathers.

There's even a day for trees.

It's called Arbor Day.

Betty: And so now you want a day, too.

Kevin: Right!

I want a day just for me.

A me day.

Hey, that's what I'll call it.

Betty: What?

Kevin: ME Day.

Betty: I couldn't think of a better name.

Kevin: That's it.

I'll have a ME Day.

Betty: Well, if you can have a ME Day,
so can I.

Kevin: Sure, why not?
That's a good idea.

Betty: Now you and I have a ME Day.
But what are we going to do
on ME Day?

Kevin: Gee, I don't know.

But how about something special

on ME Day?

Like eating popcorn all day.

Betty: How about sleeping all day?

Or camping out?

I would like that.

Kevin: Me, too.

What would you do if you had a
ME Day?

Come up with some ideas
for ME Day.

Tangletalk

One dark night the sun was bright.
I couldn't see, there was plenty of light.
So I stood sitting on a chair.
Had to! Wasn't any furniture there.

I wanted to read, so I shut the book.
Then I closed my eyes and took a look.
I noticed a bluefish walking on by,
So I decided to teach it to fly.

Austin Tighe

I Found Them in The Yellow Pages

by Norma Farber

The Car That Talked Too Much

There was a purple sports car.
And he liked to talk.

Next to the sports car lived
an old brown car.
But he never talked much at all.
He just liked to sit and think.

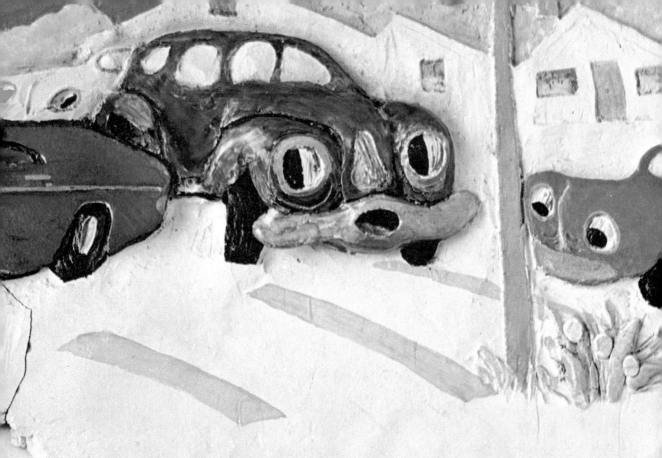

One day the new sports car called out.

"I can't find a car that can beat me.

That's how fast I am."

"Bah" said the old car.

"Who said 'Bah'?" yelled the new car.

"I did," answered the old car.

"Old car," called the sports car.
"Are you fast enough to beat me?"

"Can't say that I am,"
said the old car.
"Can't say that I'm not."

The new car just laughed and laughed.

"A race," said a truck.
"A race will tell."

"A race! A race!"
cheered all the other cars and trucks.

The two cars lined up for the race—
the new purple sports car
and the old brown car.

"The race will be to the red house
and back again," called the truck.

"May the fast car win," cheered
all the other cars and trucks.

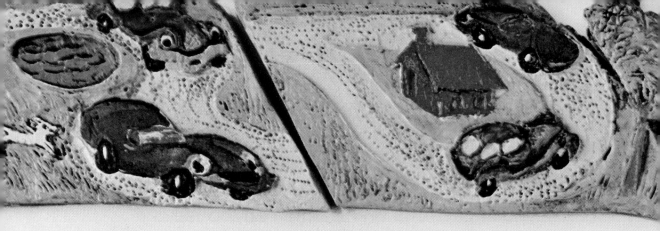

"Go!" called the truck.

Away went the purple sports car.
Away went the old brown car.

Past the pond they went.
The purple sports car was first.

Past the farmer's garden they went.
The purple sports car was still first.
"See how fast I am?" he called.

Around the red house they went.
The purple sports car was still
in front.

Now they were on their way back.

"Bah to you!"
called the purple sports car.

"I am the fastest."

Past the farmer's garden they raced.

The purple sports car was still
in front.

He turned to laugh at the old car.

But that old brown car was getting

closer,
and closer,
and closer,

Past the pond they raced.

Now the purple sports car
was not in front.

The old brown car was!

"The old brown car is going to win,"
cheered all the other cars and trucks.

And sure enough!
That old brown car did win.
He beat the new purple sports car.

"How did you do it?" asked the truck.

"How could an old car beat me?"
asked the new purple sports car.

"Maybe my new engine helped,"
said the old brown car.

Then the truck spoke.
"I guess you can't always tell
about something from the outside.
You have to look at the inside."

MAKE A CAR

46

Buying a Car

My dad is thinking
about buying a new car.

This is where cars are sold.

There are old cars and new cars.

There are big cars and little cars.

This man is called a salesman.

He will tell Dad and me
all about the cars.

They bring the new cars
on this big truck.

Then they drive the cars
off the truck.

The drivers must be careful.

Here is where
they work to fix the cars.

They work on the engine
and all the parts of the car.

New cars and old cars
are fixed here.

Here is where they keep the tools
that are used to fix the cars.

Can you tell what any
of these tools are used for?

And this is the car
that my dad bought.

And that is me sitting
in the front seat.

All on a Ride

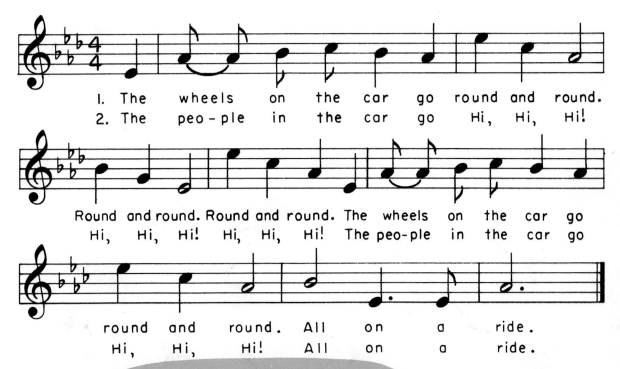

1. The wheels on the car go round and round.
2. The peo-ple in the car go Hi, Hi, Hi!

Round and round. Round and round. The wheels on the car go
Hi, Hi, Hi! Hi, Hi, Hi! The peo-ple in the car go

round and round. All on a ride.
Hi, Hi, Hi! All on a ride.

3. The radio in the car goes Do-do-de-do.
   Do-do-de-do. Do-do-de-do.
   The radio in the car goes Do-do-de-do.
   All on a ride.

4. The wipers on the car go swish, swish, swish.
   Swish, swish, swish. Swish, swish, swish.
   The wipers on the car go swish, swish, swish.
   All on a ride.

53

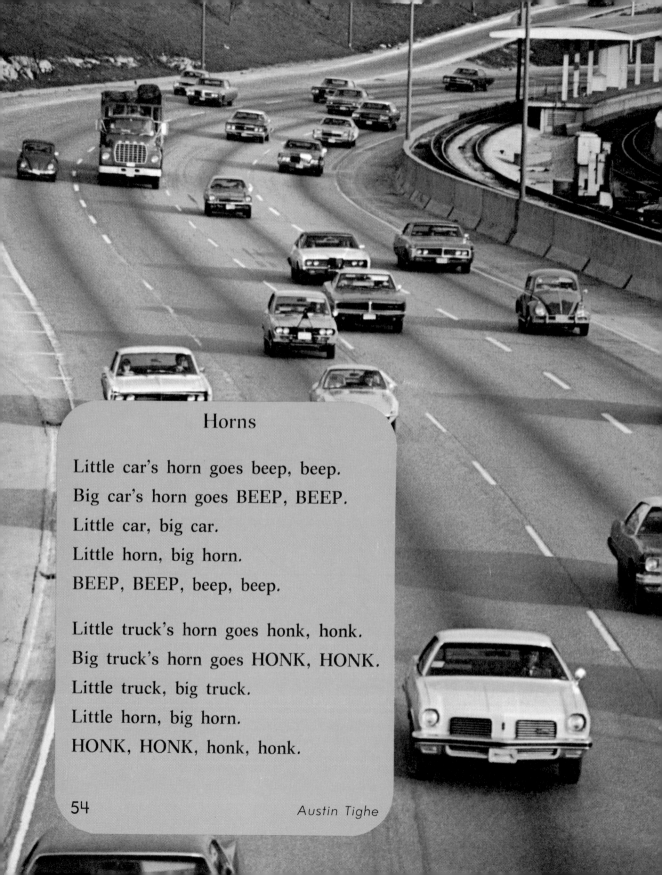

Horns

Little car's horn goes beep, beep.
Big car's horn goes BEEP, BEEP.
Little car, big car.
Little horn, big horn.
BEEP, BEEP, beep, beep.

Little truck's horn goes honk, honk.
Big truck's horn goes HONK, HONK.
Little truck, big truck.
Little horn, big horn.
HONK, HONK, honk, honk.

54   Austin Tighe

The Power Shovel

The power digger
Is much bigger
　　Than the biggest beast I know!
He snorts and roars
Like the dinosaurs
　　That lived long years ago.

He crouches low
　　On his tractor paws
And scoops the dirt up
　　With his jaws;
Then swings his long
　　Stiff neck around
And spits it out
　　Upon the ground...

Rowena Bennett

ABC of Cars
and Trucks
by Anne Alexander

What Happens Next?

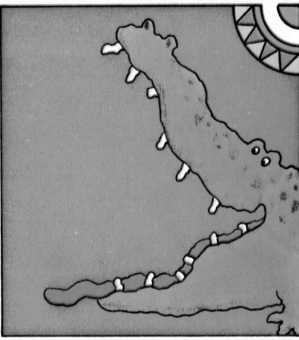

Head Over Tail

One day Riley was running
with the other puppies.
Around and around
Riley raced.

But his back legs ran too fast.
And his front legs ran too slow.
So over he would go.
Head over tail!

All at once Riley saw
that the gate was open.
He ran to it.

Riley looked up the street.
No one was there.
Riley looked down the street.
No one was there.
So out went Riley.

Soon Riley came to another open gate.

Inside he saw a yard.

So he ran in to play.

A woman in a big hat came out
of the house.

She saw Riley.

"Go away, little dog!

Don't you get in my garden!"

Riley ran out of the yard.

His back legs ran too fast.

And his front legs ran too slow.

Over he went.

Head over tail!

Riley ran on down the street.

Then he stopped.

He heard something.

He ran behind some bushes.

Riley looked out.

And he saw a little girl.

But the little girl

didn't see Riley.

So the girl walked right by.

Riley jumped out.

He barked at the little girl.

"Bow-wow! Bow-wow!"

Riley ran after the little girl.

But his back legs ran too fast.

And his front legs ran too slow.

Over he flipped.

Head over tail!

Riley and his new friend played
for a long time.

After a time the girl stopped.
"I am going in now," she said.
"I'll tell Mother and Dad about you."

Riley sat and waited.
He cried just a little.
But he stayed and waited
for the girl.

A man came walking by.

He saw Riley sitting and waiting.

"Come here, little dog,"
he said.

"Let's see who you are."

The man looked at Riley's tag.

"Well, you're Mr. Barker's dog,"
he said.

"Back you go."

And he took Riley into his arms.

Riley was soon back in Mr. Barker's yard.

And he was now very sleepy.

He had played hard
with his new friend.

Just then he heard voices.

One was the voice of his new friend.

The other was Mr. Barker's voice.

"Would you like to have him?"
Mr. Barker asked.

"Riley is old enough
to leave his mother now."

"Wow!" was all the girl could say.

"Bow-wow!" barked Riley.

As if to say, "And how!"

66

Tricks

What tricks would you teach the animals?

Animal Tracks

Buck put food in a dish
for his cat.
Keekee put food in a dish
for her dog.

But the cat never got the cat food.
And the dog never got the dog food.

Who got the cat's food?
Who got the dog's food?

DOG   CAT

Look first at the tracks
to the cat's food.

They were made by
an animal with four feet.

A cat has four feet.

And claws!

But a dog has four feet
and claws, too.

Now, who went to the cat's food?

You don't know?

Look again!

69

Now look at the other tracks.

The tracks to the dog's dish.

The footprints are in one line.

They are made by some animal.

It was an animal that looks as though
it walked on two feet.

And no claws show!

What can it be?

If you can, watch how a cat walks.

A cat walks on four feet.
But watch where his two back feet go.
They go right in the tracks
of his front feet.
His footprints are in a line.
One is right in back of the other.
They look like the footprints
of an animal with just two feet.

Watch again when a cat walks.

See how he pulls in his front

and his back claws?

That's why you can't see claw marks.

Cat footprints have no claw marks.

Now do you know?

Who got the cat's food?

Who got the dog's food?

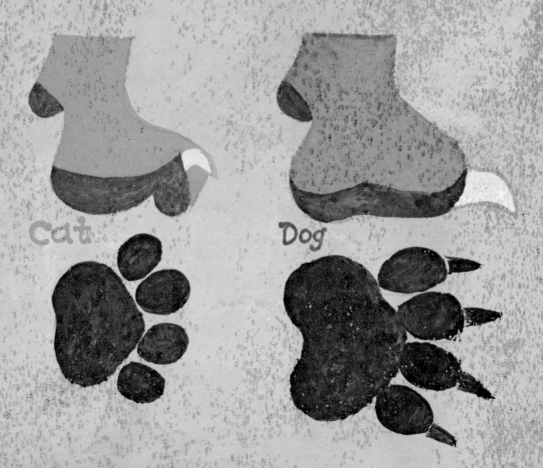

Cat

Dog

An animal detective finds tracks.

He looks everywhere for them.

In the front yard.

In the backyard.

Around his house.

Near a pond.

Everywhere.

He is always on the watch.

See if you can match the tracks with the
animal that made them.

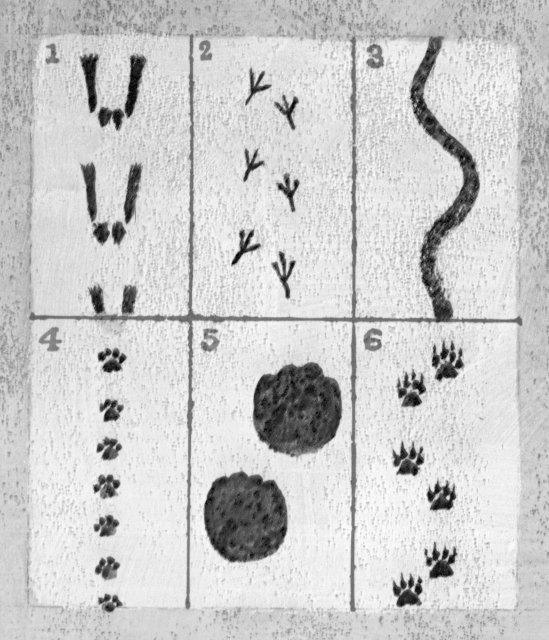

Paper Clip Trick

Try this paper clip trick.

1 Use paper and two paper clips.

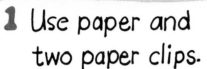

2 Do this to the paper.

3 Put paper clips on the paper.

4 Pull on the ends of the paper.

What happens to the paper clips?

Out and In

There were two skunks—
    Out and In.
When In was out,
    Out was in.
One day Out was in
    and In was out.
Their mother,
    who was in with Out,
    wanted In in.
"Bring In in,"
    she said to Out.
So Out went out
    and brought In in.
"How did you find him
    so fast?" she asked.
"Instinct," he said.

Midnight

CLANG! CLANG! CLANG!

The fire truck
came down the street.

The fire truck stopped,
right in front of a big old house.
Smoke was coming out of the windows.

78

A policeman was trying

to keep everyone back.

One fireman was on the truck.

"Who is in the house?" he called.

"No one," answered another fireman.

"No one is living here."

The firemen worked hard.
They put their ladders up.
But they could not put the fire out.

Smoke was coming out
of every window now.

CLANG! CLANG! CLANG!

More fire trucks came.
A policeman yelled,
"Get back, everyone."

All at once someone yelled,
"Look up there!
   In that window!"

High up in one of the windows
sat a black cat.

"That's Midnight!" yelled a girl.
"He lives in that old building.
I'm going in and save him!"
And the girl began to run.

"No, you're not," said a policeman.

He stopped the girl.

"Yell to the cat.

Get him to jump down.

We will catch him."

"Jump, Midnight!"

yelled the boys and girls below.

"Jump!"

But Midnight would not jump.

He was too scared.

Smoke was coming out of the window.

All around Midnight.

"Quick!" yelled a fireman.

"Put up a ladder.

Right to the window."

In no time another ladder was going up.

and UP! and UP!

Right to the window.

A fireman ran up the ladder.

He got to the window.

He reached out.

And he grabbed Midnight.

Everyone below cheered.

The fireman was down with Midnight.

But Midnight had no home now.
No place to go.

"I'll take him," said the fire chief.
"He can be the firehouse cat.
And live in the firehouse.
And ride the fire truck."

CLANG! CLANG! CLANG!

The fire truck went away
down the street.

"Meow!" said Midnight,
the firehouse cat!
As he sat right in front,
with the fire chief.

What Happens Next?

Frog and Toad Together

by Arnold Lobel

The Ocean

The ocean is very big.
Close to the land,
the water is not deep.
But away from the land,
the water can be very deep.

People have sailed boats on the ocean
for a long time.

But they could not go deep
into the water.

They did not have underwater boats.

So they did not know much
about the deep ocean.

Then people began to swim deeper
into the ocean.

At first, they could not go very deep.

They did not have enough air.

And the water was too cold.

So they built underwater boats.

One kind of boat was called
a bathysphere.

It was made like a steel ball.

Two people could ride
in the bathysphere.

There was air in the bathysphere.

Now people could go down
into the deep ocean.

The boat would keep out the water.

From inside the steel ball,
people learned many things.

They learned that all the water
in the ocean is not the same.

The water in the deep part
of the ocean is cold.

The water above it is warm.

There are plants and fish
in the warm water.

And there are fish
in the cold, deep water.

But they are not the same.

Deep in the ocean,
the water is black.
It is hard to see
from the underwater boat.
But the people in it can see
the fish swimming by.
They have spots of light—
on their bodies,
on their heads,
and under their mouths.

Much has been learned
about the ocean.

But there is still
much to be learned.

People will go deep into the ocean
again and again.

They will try to find out
all they can.

They will study the plants and fishes
of the ocean.

They will study the water.

And they will study the land
under the ocean.

We use the plants and fish for food.
But soon we will want to use more.

We use the oil
that is under the ocean.
But soon we will want to use more.

The ocean can help us
if we know how to use it.
And if we use it carefully.

WHALES

The largest animal lives in the ocean.

It is a whale.

The largest animal that has ever lived

is the blue whale.

If you ever, ever, ever, ever, ever meet a whale,

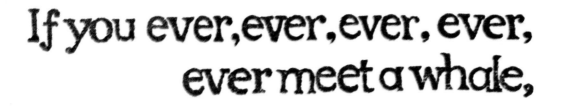

You must never, never, never, never
grab him by his tail.
If you ever, ever, ever, ever
grab him by his tail—
You will never, never, never, never
meet another whale.

Traditional Rhyme

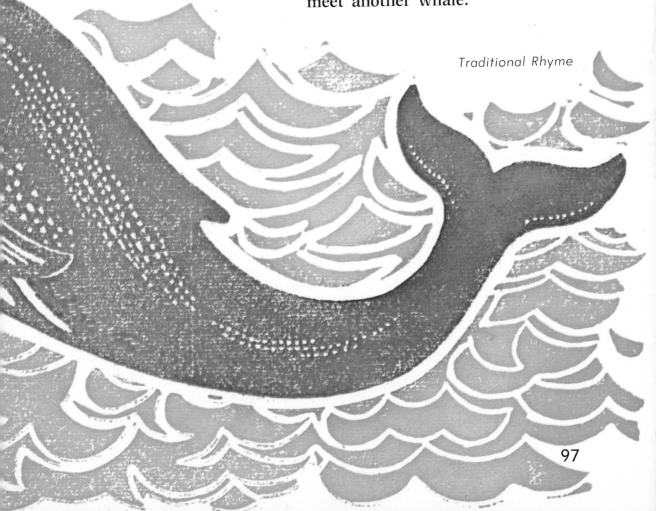

Elephants

The largest animal that lives on land is the elephant.

An elephant can't jump at all because its legs are so heavy.

A Hose
For A Nose

An elephant's size is grand,

Much the biggest thing on land.

And especially long is its nose,

Which resembles a garden hose.

So if an elephant catches cold,

And it begins to sneeze,

Remember what you've been told,

And run for cover—please.

Austin Tighe

Make an Aquarium

In an aquarium you can study fish.
You will be able to learn
about how they live.

Here is what you will need
for your aquarium.

glass case

water

fish

fish food

sand

small rocks

plants

snails

Step 1

Step 2

Step 3

Step 4

Step 5

Step 6

Now study the fish in the aquarium.

The Listening Walk
by Paul Showers

Katy-did-it

Katy ran to get her new book.

Crash!

Down came Grandma's lamp.

All in pieces.

Just then little Tom
came into the room
on his little red truck.

Katy heard Grandma coming.

So she ran outside.

Then she heard Grandma say,

"Tom! Look what you did!

My best lamp!

All in pieces!"

"That's good," thought Katy.

"Now Grandma will never know
I broke her lamp.

Tom can't tell.

He's too little."

So Katy ran off to play.

She stayed out
until she heard Grandma call.

"Come in now, Katy.

Dinner is ready."

At dinner Grandma looked sad.

"Tom broke my best lamp," she said.

Katy didn't say a thing.

"I can't tell now," she thought.

"Not until after dinner.

Grandma would get upset."

But Katy had a hard time
eating her dinner.

At bedtime Tom came to Katy.

Katy wanted to say "Good night."

But she had a hard time
not crying.

She wanted to tell Grandma
about the lamp.

But she just couldn't—
not then.

At last it was Katy's bedtime.
And she was glad.

"Goodnight, Grandma," she said.
She went into her room,
right next to Grandma's.

Katy looked at the big tree
outside her window.
She looked at the round yellow
moon above.
Then she got into bed.

In the night Katy heard something.

Like someone said,

Katy-did-it

Katy put her head
way down under the covers.
But she heard it again!

Katy-did-it

And again.

Katy-did-it

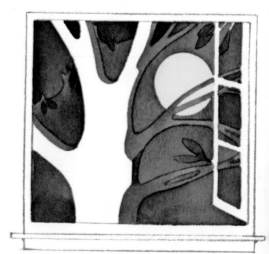

Katy-did-it

"Someone knows," thought Katy.

"I wish they would stop."

But they didn't.

Katy-did-it
Katy-did-it
Katy-did-it

Over and over Katy heard it.

At last Katy cried out,

"Stop!

Please stop saying that!"

And Katy jumped out of bed.

What do you think Katy did then?

What had Katy heard?

Sometimes Things Happen

You know how things happen sometimes.
You don't want them to happen.
But they do.

And sometimes you get in trouble
because things happen.
Things that you didn't want to happen.
Let me tell you about yesterday.

Yesterday was a bad, bad day—
all because of Randy.

Randy is just about my best friend.

Or I thought he was.

Randy and I always walk to school
together.

Or sometimes we run to school.

Or race to school.

Or play tag on the way to school.

Yesterday we played tag
on the way to school.
I was "It."
I had to catch Randy.
He ran in front of me.
There were some kids walking.
Randy bumped into one of them.
It was Lisa, a girl in our class.

I was running right behind Randy.

I saw him bump into Lisa.

I saw Lisa fall.

I ran up next to Lisa.

Lisa looked up at me.

She was crying and

her leg was cut.

I put out my hand to help Lisa up.

"Get away from me, Terry," she yelled.

"You're the one who bumped me."

I began to tell her that it wasn't me.

That it was Randy who did it.

But I looked around and

Randy wasn't there.

He must have kept on running.

Lisa was still crying when we got to school.

She went right up to Mrs. Keenan, our teacher.

She told her what had happened.

She told Mrs. Keenan that I had bumped into her.

I heard her.

Now I knew that I was in trouble.

I looked around and saw Randy.

He was in his seat.

He didn't look at me.

But I knew that he had heard Lisa, too.

Mrs. Keenan called me to her desk.

I knew she would.

And I knew what she was going to ask me.

But there was something I didn't know.

I didn't know how I was going to answer.

What do you think Mrs. Keenan will ask?

What do you think Terry will answer?

What would you tell if this happened to you?

Brave Daniel

by Leonore Klein